EMMANUEL JOSEPH

Aid in Arms, The Intersection of Humanitarian Efforts and Military Strategy

Copyright © 2025 by Emmanuel Joseph

All rights reserved. No part of this publication may be reproduced, stored or transmitted in any form or by any means, electronic, mechanical, photocopying, recording, scanning, or otherwise without written permission from the publisher. It is illegal to copy this book, post it to a website, or distribute it by any other means without permission.

First edition

This book was professionally typeset on Reedsy.
Find out more at reedsy.com

Contents

1. Chapter 1 — 1
2. Chapter 1: The Genesis of Humanitarian-Military Synergy — 3
3. Chapter 2: The Evolution of Joint Operations — 5
4. Chapter 3: Navigating the Ethical and Moral Dilemmas — 7
5. Chapter 4: Case Studies in Humanitarian-Military... — 9
6. Chapter 5: The Role of International Organizations — 11
7. Chapter 6: The Impact of Technology on Humanitarian-Military... — 13
8. Chapter 7: The Role of Local Actors — 15
9. Chapter 8: The Challenges of Coordination and Communication — 17
10. Chapter 9: The Impact of Humanitarian-Military Collaboration... — 19
11. Chapter 10: The Future of Humanitarian-Military... — 21
12. Chapter 11: Lessons Learned and Best Practices — 23
13. Chapter 12: Conclusion: The Path Forward — 25

1

Chapter 1

Introduction

The convergence of humanitarian aid and military strategy is a complex and multifaceted phenomenon, reflecting the evolving nature of global crises and the responses they necessitate. Historically, humanitarian efforts have been guided by principles of neutrality, impartiality, and independence, while military strategies have focused on defense, security, and combat operations. However, the increasing prevalence of complex emergencies—where humanitarian needs and security concerns are inextricably linked—has necessitated a more integrated approach. This book explores the intricate relationship between humanitarian aid and military strategy, examining the historical context, ethical dilemmas, and practical implications of their intersection.

The need for humanitarian-military collaboration has become increasingly evident in the face of modern crises. Natural disasters, armed conflicts, and public health emergencies have demonstrated that neither humanitarian organizations nor military forces can address these challenges in isolation. The synergy between these two sectors allows for a more comprehensive and effective response, ensuring that aid reaches those in need while maintaining security and stability. This introduction will provide an overview of the key themes and issues that will be explored in the subsequent chapters, setting the stage for a deeper understanding of the complexities involved in humanitarian-military collaboration.

One of the central themes of this book is the ethical and moral dilemmas that arise from the intersection of humanitarian aid and military strategy. Balancing humanitarian principles with military objectives presents a significant challenge, as the priorities and methodologies of these two sectors can often conflict. This introduction will highlight some of the key ethical considerations that will be examined in greater detail, such as the potential for humanitarian efforts to be co-opted for military purposes and the importance of preserving humanitarian space. By addressing these dilemmas, the book aims to provide a nuanced perspective on the delicate balance that must be maintained in humanitarian-military collaboration.

The role of international organizations, local actors, and technology in shaping humanitarian-military collaboration is another critical aspect that will be explored in this book. International organizations such as the United Nations and the International Committee of the Red Cross play a pivotal role in facilitating dialogue and cooperation between humanitarian and military actors. Local actors, including community organizations and individuals, bring invaluable knowledge and resources to joint efforts. Technological advancements, from satellite imagery to mobile apps, have transformed the way humanitarian and military actors operate in the field. This introduction will provide a brief overview of these key players and their contributions to humanitarian-military collaboration.

As we delve into the complexities of humanitarian-military collaboration, it is essential to recognize the importance of continuous learning and adaptation. Each crisis presents unique challenges and opportunities, offering valuable lessons and insights that can inform future efforts. This book aims to compile these lessons and best practices, providing a comprehensive and insightful exploration of the intersection of humanitarian aid and military strategy. By examining the historical context, ethical dilemmas, and practical implications of this collaboration, the book seeks to contribute to a more effective and principled approach to addressing global crises.

2

Chapter 1: The Genesis of Humanitarian-Military Synergy

The convergence of humanitarian aid and military strategy is a relatively modern phenomenon. Tracing its origins back to the post-World War II era, the concept began taking shape when the lines between combatant and civilian became increasingly blurred. In the aftermath of immense devastation, the rebuilding process required a multifaceted approach, blending relief efforts with security measures. As various global crises unfolded, the importance of cooperation between humanitarian organizations and military forces became evident. This chapter will delve into the historical context and early instances that laid the groundwork for this partnership.

Initially, these two entities operated in distinct spheres, with humanitarian agencies focusing solely on alleviating human suffering and the military prioritizing defense and combat operations. However, as conflicts grew more complex and widespread, the necessity for a united front became undeniable. The early interactions between these groups were marked by tension and mistrust, as each had its own set of priorities and methodologies. This chapter will examine the challenges and breakthroughs in forging a cooperative relationship, shedding light on key events that signified the beginning of this unlikely alliance.

Key players in this nascent collaboration included international organizations like the United Nations, Red Cross, and various non-governmental organizations (NGOs). Their collective experiences in war-torn regions highlighted the need for coordinated efforts to ensure the safety and well-being of affected populations. This chapter will explore the roles played by these organizations in shaping the discourse around humanitarian-military cooperation and how their contributions were instrumental in setting the stage for future endeavors.

One of the most significant developments during this period was the establishment of guidelines and protocols for collaboration. These frameworks aimed to bridge the gap between humanitarian principles and military objectives, ensuring that both parties could work together effectively without compromising their core values. This chapter will discuss the creation and evolution of these guidelines, highlighting key documents and agreements that have shaped the field.

As the chapter concludes, it will reflect on the lessons learned from these early experiences and how they have influenced contemporary practices. The initial steps taken towards integrating humanitarian aid and military strategy have paved the way for more sophisticated and nuanced approaches, setting the stage for the complex dynamics that define today's humanitarian-military partnerships.

3

Chapter 2: The Evolution of Joint Operations

The relationship between humanitarian organizations and military forces has evolved significantly over the past few decades. As global conflicts have grown more intricate and multifaceted, the need for collaborative efforts has become increasingly apparent. This chapter will explore the progression of joint operations, examining how both sectors have adapted to the changing landscape and developed more cohesive strategies for working together.

In the early stages of joint operations, there were numerous obstacles to overcome. Humanitarian organizations often viewed military involvement with suspicion, fearing that their presence would undermine the impartiality and neutrality essential to their work. Conversely, military forces were wary of the perceived inefficiency and idealism of humanitarian agencies. This chapter will delve into the initial challenges faced by both parties and how they gradually began to understand the value of each other's contributions.

A significant turning point in the evolution of joint operations was the recognition that humanitarian crises could not be addressed solely through either aid or military intervention. Complex emergencies, such as those in Rwanda, Bosnia, and Somalia, demonstrated the need for a more integrated approach. This chapter will analyze these case studies, highlighting the lessons learned and how they influenced subsequent joint operations.

The development of joint training programs and exercises played a crucial role in fostering better collaboration between humanitarian and military actors. These initiatives aimed to bridge the cultural and operational divide, enabling both parties to work more effectively together in the field. This chapter will discuss the various training programs implemented over the years, their impact on joint operations, and how they have contributed to a more seamless integration of efforts.

As the chapter draws to a close, it will reflect on the current state of joint operations and the ongoing challenges that need to be addressed. Despite significant progress, there remain areas where improvement is needed, particularly in ensuring that humanitarian principles are upheld in the context of military involvement. The chapter will conclude with a forward-looking perspective, considering the future of humanitarian-military collaboration and the potential for further advancements.

4

Chapter 3: Navigating the Ethical and Moral Dilemmas

The intersection of humanitarian efforts and military strategy is fraught with ethical and moral dilemmas. Balancing the principles of neutrality, impartiality, and independence with the strategic objectives of military operations presents a complex and often contentious challenge. This chapter will delve into the various ethical considerations that arise in the context of humanitarian-military collaboration, exploring the delicate balance that must be maintained to ensure that both humanitarian and military objectives are met without compromising core values.

One of the primary ethical concerns in humanitarian-military collaboration is the potential for humanitarian efforts to be co-opted for military purposes. This chapter will examine instances where aid has been used as a tool for achieving military objectives, often at the expense of the affected populations. The discussion will focus on the implications of such practices and the measures that have been put in place to prevent the misuse of humanitarian aid.

Another significant ethical dilemma is the potential for humanitarian organizations to be perceived as taking sides in a conflict. The principles of neutrality and impartiality are essential to maintaining the trust and confidence of affected populations and warring parties. This chapter will explore the challenges faced by humanitarian organizations in maintaining these principles while working alongside military forces and the strategies they employ to navigate this complex terrain.

The concept of "humanitarian space" is central to the ethical considerations in humanitarian-military collaboration. This chapter will discuss the importance of preserving this space and the potential risks posed by military involvement. The discussion will include an analysis of how humanitarian organizations and military forces can work together to ensure that humanitarian space is respected and protected.

As the chapter concludes, it will reflect on the lessons learned from navigating these ethical and moral dilemmas and the ongoing efforts to strike a balance between humanitarian principles and military objectives. The chapter will consider the potential for future advancements in ethical frameworks and the role that both humanitarian organizations and military forces can play in fostering a more principled and effective collaboration.

5

Chapter 4: Case Studies in Humanitarian-Military Collaboration

C ase studies provide valuable insights into the practical application of humanitarian-military collaboration. This chapter will examine several notable instances of joint efforts, highlighting the successes, challenges, and lessons learned from each case. By analyzing these real-world examples, we can better understand the dynamics at play and the factors that contribute to effective collaboration.

One of the most well-documented case studies is the response to the 2004 Indian Ocean tsunami. This chapter will explore how humanitarian organizations and military forces from various countries came together to provide relief and support to the affected populations. The discussion will focus on the coordination mechanisms that were put in place, the challenges faced in the field, and the lessons learned from this large-scale disaster response.

Another significant case study is the humanitarian response to the conflict in Afghanistan. This chapter will analyze the collaboration between humanitarian organizations and military forces in a complex and volatile environment. The discussion will highlight the strategies employed to navigate the challenges of working in a conflict zone, the ethical considerations at play, and the impact of military involvement on humanitarian efforts.

The response to the Ebola outbreak in West Africa is another critical case study in humanitarian-military collaboration. This chapter will examine how humanitarian organizations and military forces worked together to contain the outbreak and provide medical care to affected populations. The discussion will focus on the unique challenges posed by a public health crisis, the role of military forces in supporting humanitarian efforts, and the lessons learned from this unprecedented response.

As the chapter concludes, it will reflect on the common themes and lessons that emerge from these case studies. The discussion will consider the factors that contribute to successful collaboration, the challenges that need to be addressed, and the potential for future advancements in humanitarian-military efforts. By examining these real-world examples, we can gain a deeper understanding of the complexities and nuances of humanitarian-military collaboration and the potential for positive outcomes.

6

Chapter 5: The Role of International Organizations

International organizations play a critical role in facilitating humanitarian-military collaboration. This chapter will explore the contributions of key international actors, such as the United Nations, the International Committee of the Red Cross, and various non-governmental organizations (NGOs), in shaping the discourse and practice of humanitarian-military efforts.

The United Nations has been at the forefront of promoting and coordinating humanitarian-military collaboration. This chapter will examine the various UN agencies and initiatives that have been instrumental in fostering cooperation between humanitarian and military actors. The discussion will focus on the development of guidelines and protocols, the role of the UN in coordinating joint efforts, and the impact of these initiatives on the ground.

The International Committee of the Red Cross (ICRC) is another key player in humanitarian-military collaboration. This chapter will explore the unique position of the ICRC as a neutral and impartial organization and its role in facilitating dialogue and cooperation between humanitarian and military actors. The discussion will highlight the ICRC's contributions to the development of ethical frameworks and the preservation of humanitarian space.

Non-governmental organizations (NGOs) also play a vital role in humanitarian-military collaboration. This chapter will examine the contributions of various NGOs in promoting and implementing joint efforts, the challenges they face in working with military forces, and the strategies they employ to navigate these challenges. The discussion will consider the unique perspectives and strengths that NGOs bring to the table and their impact on the overall effectiveness of humanitarian-military efforts.

As the chapter concludes, it will reflect on the importance of international organizations in shaping the landscape of humanitarian-military collaboration. The discussion will consider the ongoing efforts to strengthen these partnerships, the potential for future advancements, and the role that international organizations can play in fostering a more effective and principled collaboration.

7

Chapter 6: The Impact of Technology on Humanitarian-Military Collaboration

The advent of new technologies has had a profound impact on humanitarian-military collaboration. From advanced communication systems to innovative data collection methods, technology has transformed the way humanitarian and military actors work together. This chapter will explore the various technological advancements that have influenced humanitarian-military efforts and the potential for future innovations.

One of the most significant technological advancements has been the development of satellite imagery and remote sensing. These tools have revolutionized the way humanitarian organizations and military forces assess and respond to crises. This chapter will discuss how satellite imagery has been used to monitor conflict zones, track population movements, and assess the impact of natural disasters. The discussion will also consider the ethical implications of using such technologies and the measures in place to ensure their responsible use.

The rise of mobile technology has also had a significant impact on humanitarian-military collaboration. Mobile phones and apps have enabled better communication and coordination between humanitarian organizations, military forces, and affected populations. This chapter will explore how mobile technology has been used to disseminate information, provide early warning systems, and facilitate data collection in the field. The discussion will highlight the successes and challenges of implementing mobile technology in humanitarian-military efforts.

Drones have emerged as another valuable tool in humanitarian-military operations. This chapter will examine the various applications of drone technology, from delivering aid to remote areas to conducting aerial surveys and assessments. The discussion will consider the benefits and limitations of using drones in humanitarian contexts and the potential for further advancements in this field.

As the chapter concludes, it will reflect on the potential for future technological innovations to enhance humanitarian-military collaboration. The discussion will consider emerging technologies, such as artificial intelligence and blockchain, and their potential applications in humanitarian-military efforts. The chapter will also consider the importance of ensuring that technological advancements are used responsibly and ethically, with a focus on promoting the well-being of affected populations.

8

Chapter 7: The Role of Local Actors

Local actors play a crucial role in the success of humanitarian-military collaboration. This chapter will explore the contributions of local organizations, communities, and individuals in shaping and implementing joint efforts. The discussion will highlight the importance of engaging with local actors and the benefits of leveraging their knowledge, skills, and resources.

Local organizations often have a deep understanding of the cultural, social, and political context in which they operate. This chapter will examine how humanitarian and military actors can work with local organizations to ensure that their efforts are culturally sensitive and contextually appropriate. The discussion will highlight the importance of building trust and fostering strong relationships with local actors to enhance the effectiveness of joint operations.

Community engagement is another critical aspect of humanitarian-military collaboration. This chapter will explore the various strategies used to involve local communities in the planning and implementation of joint efforts. The discussion will consider the benefits of community engagement, such as increased ownership and sustainability of projects, as well as the challenges and limitations that may arise.

The role of local individuals, including community leaders and volunteers, is also essential in humanitarian-military efforts. This chapter will highlight the contributions of these individuals and the impact they have on the success of joint operations. The discussion will consider the importance of recognizing and supporting the efforts of local individuals, as well as the potential for capacity-building and empowerment.

As the chapter concludes, it will reflect on the lessons learned from engaging with local actors and the ongoing efforts to strengthen these partnerships. The discussion will consider the potential for future advancements in local engagement and the role that both humanitarian organizations and military forces can play in fostering a more inclusive and effective collaboration.

9

Chapter 8: The Challenges of Coordination and Communication

Effective coordination and communication are critical to the success of humanitarian-military collaboration. This chapter will explore the various challenges faced in coordinating joint efforts and the strategies employed to overcome these obstacles. The discussion will highlight the importance of clear communication, mutual understanding, and effective coordination mechanisms in ensuring the success of joint operations.

One of the primary challenges in humanitarian-military coordination is the differing organizational cultures and operational priorities. This chapter will examine the impact of these differences on joint efforts and the strategies used to bridge the cultural divide. The discussion will consider the importance of building mutual understanding and respect between humanitarian and military actors to enhance collaboration.

Communication barriers, such as language differences and varying communication styles, can also pose significant challenges in humanitarian-military efforts. This chapter will explore the impact of these barriers on joint operations and the measures taken to improve communication. The discussion will highlight the importance of effective communication in building trust, fostering cooperation, and ensuring the success of joint efforts.

Coordination mechanisms, such as joint planning and information-sharing platforms, play a crucial role in facilitating humanitarian-military collaboration. This chapter will discuss the various coordination mechanisms used in the field and their impact on joint operations. The discussion will consider the benefits and limitations of these mechanisms and the potential for further improvements.

As the chapter concludes, it will reflect on the lessons learned from addressing the challenges of coordination and communication in humanitarian-military efforts. The discussion will consider the ongoing efforts to enhance coordination and communication and the potential for future advancements in this area. The chapter will also consider the importance of fostering a culture of collaboration and mutual understanding to ensure the success of joint operations.

10

Chapter 9: The Impact of Humanitarian-Military Collaboration on Affected Populations

The primary goal of humanitarian-military collaboration is to improve the well-being of affected populations. This chapter will explore the impact of joint efforts on the communities and individuals they aim to support. The discussion will consider the benefits and potential drawbacks of humanitarian-military collaboration and the importance of ensuring that the needs and rights of affected populations are prioritized.

One of the key benefits of humanitarian-military collaboration is the ability to provide timely and effective assistance in crises. This chapter will examine the various ways in which joint efforts have enhanced the delivery of aid and support to affected populations. The discussion will highlight the successes and challenges of these efforts and the factors that contribute to their effectiveness.

However, there are also potential drawbacks to humanitarian-military collaboration. This chapter will explore the potential risks and negative impacts of joint efforts on affected populations, such as the blurring of lines between humanitarian and military actors and the potential for aid to be perceived as biased or politicized. The discussion will consider the measures taken to mitigate these risks and ensure that humanitarian principles are upheld.

The importance of involving affected populations in the planning and implementation of humanitarian-military efforts cannot be overstated. This chapter will discuss the various strategies used to engage with communities and individuals, ensuring that their voices are heard and their needs are met. The discussion will highlight the benefits of community engagement and the challenges that may arise in this process.

As the chapter concludes, it will reflect on the lessons learned from the impact of humanitarian-military collaboration on affected populations. The discussion will consider the ongoing efforts to prioritize the needs and rights of affected populations and the potential for future advancements in this area. The chapter will also consider the importance of fostering a culture of accountability and transparency in humanitarian-military efforts to ensure that the well-being of affected populations remains the top priority.

11

Chapter 10: The Future of Humanitarian-Military Collaboration

As the world continues to face complex and multifaceted crises, the need for effective humanitarian-military collaboration is more important than ever. This chapter will explore the potential future of joint efforts, considering the emerging trends, challenges, and opportunities that may shape the landscape of humanitarian-military collaboration in the coming years.

One of the key trends shaping the future of humanitarian-military collaboration is the increasing emphasis on localization. This chapter will discuss the importance of empowering local actors and communities in humanitarian-military efforts and the potential benefits of a more localized approach. The discussion will consider the challenges and opportunities of localization and the strategies used to promote local ownership and leadership.

Another significant trend is the growing recognition of the importance of mental health and psychosocial support in humanitarian-military efforts. This chapter will explore the various ways in which mental health and psychosocial support can be integrated into joint operations and the potential benefits of a more holistic approach. The discussion will highlight the successes and challenges of implementing mental health and psychosocial support in humanitarian-military efforts and the potential for future advancements in this area.

The impact of climate change on humanitarian-military collaboration is another critical consideration for the future. This chapter will examine the various ways in which climate change is expected to affect the nature and frequency of crises and the implications for humanitarian-military efforts. The discussion will consider the potential strategies for addressing climate-related challenges and the role that humanitarian and military actors can play in promoting climate resilience.

As the chapter concludes, it will reflect on the potential future advancements in humanitarian-military collaboration and the ongoing efforts to address emerging challenges. The discussion will consider the importance of fostering a culture of innovation, collaboration, and mutual understanding to ensure the success of joint efforts in the face of an increasingly complex and dynamic global landscape.

12

Chapter 11: Lessons Learned and Best Practices

The field of humanitarian-military collaboration is continually evolving, with each new crisis providing valuable lessons and insights. This chapter will compile the key lessons learned from past experiences and highlight the best practices that have emerged in the field. The discussion will consider the factors that contribute to successful collaboration and the strategies used to overcome common challenges.

One of the key lessons learned is the importance of building trust and mutual understanding between humanitarian and military actors. This chapter will examine the various strategies used to foster trust and collaboration, such as joint training programs, dialogue initiatives, and information-sharing platforms. The discussion will highlight the benefits of these strategies and the factors that contribute to their success.

The importance of preserving humanitarian principles and ensuring that joint efforts are guided by ethical considerations is another critical lesson. This chapter will discuss the various measures taken to uphold humanitarian principles in the context of military involvement and the challenges that may arise. The discussion will consider the role of ethical frameworks, guidelines, and protocols in ensuring that humanitarian-military collaboration remains principled and effective.

The need for flexibility and adaptability in humanitarian-military efforts is another key lesson. This chapter will explore the various strategies used to adapt to changing circumstances and address emerging challenges. The discussion will highlight the importance of flexibility in adapting to evolving situations and the strategies employed to address unforeseen challenges.

The importance of leveraging local knowledge and resources is another key lesson in humanitarian-military collaboration. This chapter will discuss the various strategies used to engage with local actors and communities, ensuring that their expertise and resources are utilized effectively. The discussion will consider the benefits of local engagement, such as increased ownership and sustainability of projects, and the challenges that may arise in this process.

As the chapter concludes, it will reflect on the key lessons learned and the best practices that have emerged in the field of humanitarian-military collaboration. The discussion will consider the ongoing efforts to improve joint operations and the potential for future advancements. The chapter will also highlight the importance of fostering a culture of continuous learning and improvement to ensure the success of humanitarian-military efforts.

13

Chapter 12: Conclusion: The Path Forward

The final chapter will provide a comprehensive overview of the key themes and insights discussed throughout the book. It will reflect on the progress made in humanitarian-military collaboration and the lessons learned from past experiences. The discussion will consider the ongoing challenges and opportunities in the field and the potential for future advancements.

One of the key themes that will be highlighted is the importance of fostering a culture of collaboration and mutual understanding between humanitarian and military actors. This chapter will emphasize the need for ongoing dialogue, joint training, and information-sharing to ensure the success of joint efforts. The discussion will consider the various strategies used to build trust and foster cooperation and the factors that contribute to their effectiveness.

The importance of preserving humanitarian principles and ensuring that joint efforts are guided by ethical considerations will also be emphasized. This chapter will discuss the various measures taken to uphold humanitarian principles in the context of military involvement and the challenges that may arise. The discussion will consider the role of ethical frameworks, guidelines, and protocols in ensuring that humanitarian-military collaboration remains principled and effective.

As the chapter concludes, it will reflect on the potential future of humanitarian-military collaboration and the ongoing efforts to address emerging challenges. The discussion will consider the importance of fostering a culture of innovation, collaboration, and mutual understanding to ensure the success of joint efforts in the face of an increasingly complex and dynamic global landscape. The chapter will also highlight the importance of continuous learning and improvement in advancing the field of humanitarian-military collaboration.

In conclusion, the book will provide a comprehensive and insightful exploration of the intersection of humanitarian efforts and military strategy. It will highlight the progress made, the lessons learned, and the best practices that have emerged in the field. The book will also consider the ongoing challenges and opportunities in humanitarian-military collaboration and the potential for future advancements. By examining the complex dynamics at play and the factors that contribute to successful joint efforts, the book will provide valuable insights for practitioners, policymakers, and scholars interested in the intersection of humanitarian aid and military strategy.

Aid in Arms: The Intersection of Humanitarian Efforts and Military Strategy

In an era of increasingly complex global crises, the convergence of humanitarian aid and military strategy has become both a necessity and a challenge. "Aid in Arms" delves into the intricate relationship between these two sectors, exploring the historical context, ethical dilemmas, and practical implications of their intersection. Through a comprehensive examination of case studies, the roles of international organizations and local actors, and the impact of technological advancements, this book provides valuable insights into the multifaceted nature of humanitarian-military collaboration.

Readers will be taken on a journey through the genesis of this synergy, from its early roots in post-World War II reconstruction efforts to the sophisticated joint operations of today. The book highlights the evolution of cooperation between humanitarian organizations and military forces, addressing the initial tensions and breakthroughs that have shaped the field. Ethical and

CHAPTER 12: CONCLUSION: THE PATH FORWARD

moral dilemmas are meticulously explored, shedding light on the challenges of balancing humanitarian principles with military objectives.

"Aid in Arms" also emphasizes the critical role of international organizations like the United Nations and the International Committee of the Red Cross in facilitating dialogue and cooperation. Local actors and communities are given due recognition for their invaluable contributions to joint efforts, highlighting the importance of engaging with those directly affected by crises. Additionally, the book examines the transformative impact of technology on humanitarian-military collaboration, from satellite imagery to mobile apps and drones.

With a forward-looking perspective, "Aid in Arms" considers the future of humanitarian-military collaboration, addressing emerging trends such as localization, mental health support, and the impact of climate change. By compiling key lessons learned and best practices, the book aims to provide a comprehensive and insightful resource for practitioners, policymakers, and scholars interested in the intersection of humanitarian aid and military strategy.

"Aid in Arms" is not just a scholarly examination but a call to action for a more effective, principled, and collaborative approach to addressing global crises. Through its in-depth analysis and practical insights, the book seeks to foster a culture of continuous learning and improvement, ensuring that humanitarian and military actors can work together to alleviate human suffering and promote peace and stability.

www.ingramcontent.com/pod-product-compliance
Lightning Source LLC
LaVergne TN
LVHW020741090526
838202LV00057BA/6166